I0605127

Slow Cooker
FAVORITES

pil
Publications International, Ltd.

Louis Weber, CEO
Publications International, Ltd.
8140 Lehigh Ave
Morton Grove, IL 60053

Pictured on the front cover: Beef Bourguignon *(page 58).*

Pictured on the back cover *(clockwise from top right):* Black Bean, Zucchini and Corn Enchiladas *(page 80),* Meatball Grinders *(page 132),* Vanilla Sour Cream Cheesecake *(page 178),* Potato Soup *(page 10)* and Greek-Style Chicken Wings with Tzatziki Sauce *(page 148).*

ISBN: 978-1-63938-947-6

Manufactured in China.

8 7 6 5 4 3 2 1

Let's get social!

 @Publications_International

 @PublicationsInternational

www.pilbooks.com

Table of Contents

Soups, Stews & Chilies

MUSHROOM-BEEF STEW

• makes 4 servings •

- 1 pound beef stew meat (1-inch cubes)
- 1 can (10½ ounces) cream of mushroom soup
- 1 package (1 pound) sliced mushrooms
- 1 package (1 ounce) dry onion soup mix
- 8 ounces uncooked egg noodles

1. Combine beef, mushroom soup, mushrooms and dry soup mix in slow cooker. Cover and cook on LOW 8 to 10 hours.
2. Cook noodles in large saucepan of salted boiling according to package directions for al dente; drain. Serve stew over noodles.

CHICKEN AND BARLEY SOUP

• makes 4 servings •

- 1 cup thinly sliced celery
- 1 medium onion, chopped
- 1 carrot, thinly sliced
- ½ cup uncooked pearl barley
- 1 clove garlic, minced
- 1 cut-up whole chicken (about 4 pounds)
- 1 tablespoon olive oil
- 2½ cups chicken broth
- 1 can (about 14 ounces) diced tomatoes
- ¾ teaspoon salt
- ½ teaspoon dried basil
- ¼ teaspoon black pepper

1. Combine celery, onion, carrot, barley and garlic in slow cooker.
2. Remove and discard skin from chicken. Separate drumsticks from thighs. Trim backbone from breasts. Save wings for another use. Heat oil in large skillet over medium-high heat; brown chicken on all sides. Place in slow cooker.
3. Add broth, tomatoes, salt, basil and pepper to slow cooker. Cover and cook on LOW 7 to 8 hours or on HIGH 4 hours or until chicken and barley are tender. Remove chicken to large cutting board; remove meat from bones. Cut chicken into bite-size pieces; discard bones. Stir chicken into soup.

BEEF AND BLACK BEAN CHILI

• makes 4 servings •

- 1 pound beef stew meat (1-inch cubes)
- Salt and black pepper
- 1 tablespoon vegetable oil
- 1 red bell pepper, chopped
- 1 green bell pepper, chopped
- 1 onion, chopped
- 1 can (about 15 ounces) black beans, rinsed and drained
- 1 can (about 14 ounces) fire-roasted diced tomatoes
- 2 tablespoons chili powder
- 1 tablespoon minced garlic
- 2 teaspoons ground cumin
- ½ ounce semisweet chocolate, chopped
- 1 cup uncooked rice, cooked according to package directions
- Shredded Cheddar cheese (optional)

1 Season beef all over with salt and black pepper. Heat oil in large skillet over medium-high heat. Add beef; cook 5 minutes or until browned on all sides, turning occasionally. Transfer to slow cooker.

2 Stir in bell peppers, onion, beans, tomatoes, chili powder, garlic and cumin. Cover and cook on LOW 8 to 9 hours or until beef is very tender. Turn off heat; stir in chocolate until melted. Season to taste with additional salt and black pepper. Serve over rice; top with cheese.

POTATO SOUP

• makes 8 servings •

8 slices bacon, chopped
1 large onion, chopped
2 stalks celery, chopped
2 carrots, chopped
3 cloves garlic, minced
1 teaspoon dried thyme
5 potatoes (about 3 pounds), cut into ½-inch cubes
4 cups vegetable or chicken broth
1 cup half-and-half
1 teaspoon salt
¼ teaspoon black pepper

1 Heat large skillet over medium heat. Add bacon; cook and stir until crisp. Transfer to paper towel-lined plate using slotted spoon. Place half of bacon in slow cooker. Refrigerate remaining bacon in small bowl until ready to serve.

2 Pour off all but 2 tablespoons drippings from skillet; return to medium-high heat. Add onion, celery, carrots, garlic and thyme; cook and stir 5 to 6 minutes or until slightly softened.

3 Stir onion mixture, potatoes and broth into slow cooker. Cover and cook on LOW 7 to 8 hours or on HIGH 3 to 4 hours.

4 Mash potatoes with potato masher; stir in half-and-half, salt and pepper. Cover and cook on HIGH 15 minutes. Garnish with reserved bacon.

PESTO, WHITE BEAN AND PASTA STEW

• makes 6 servings •

- 1 can (28 ounces) Italian seasoned diced tomatoes
- 2 cups vegetable broth
- 1 green bell pepper, chopped
- 1 cup uncooked elbow macaroni or ditalini pasta
- 1 can (about 15 ounces) cannellini or Great Northern beans, rinsed and drained
- ¼ cup pesto sauce
- Salt and black pepper
- Grated Parmesan cheese

1 Spray inside of slow cooker with nonstick cooking spray. Combine tomatoes, broth, bell pepper and pasta in slow cooker; stir to blend. Cover and cook on LOW 4 to 5 hours or on HIGH 2 to 2½ hours.

2 Stir in beans and pesto. Cover and cook on HIGH 10 to 15 minutes or until heated through. Season to taste with salt and black pepper. Garnish with cheese.

FRENCH LENTIL RICE SOUP

• makes 4 servings •

- 6 cups vegetable broth
- 1 cup dried lentils, rinsed and sorted
- 2 carrots, finely diced
- 1 onion, finely chopped
- 2 stalks celery, finely diced
- 3 tablespoons uncooked rice
- 2 teaspoons minced garlic
- 1 teaspoon herbes de Provence
- ½ teaspoon salt
- ⅛ teaspoon black pepper
- 4 tablespoons whipping cream or sour cream
- ¼ cup chopped fresh parsley

1 Combine broth, lentils, carrots, onion, celery, rice, garlic, herbes de Provence, salt and pepper in slow cooker; mix well. Cover and cook on LOW 8 hours or on HIGH 4 hours.

2 Transfer about 1½ cups soup to blender or food processor; blend until almost smooth. Return to slow cooker; stir until blended. Top each serving with cream and parsley.

GREEN AND YELLOW SPLIT PEA SOUP

• makes 4 to 5 servings •

- 1 to 2 smoked ham hocks or meaty ham bones
- 6 cups water
- ¾ cup dried green split peas, rinsed and sorted
- ¾ cup dried yellow split peas, rinsed and sorted
- 1 package dry vegetable soup mix
- 1 teaspoon chicken bouillon granules *or* 1 chicken bouillon cube
- 1 bay leaf
- ½ teaspoon lemon-pepper

1 Combine ham hocks, water, peas, dry soup mix, bouillon granules, bay leaf and lemon-pepper in slow cooker. Cover and cook on LOW 4 to 5 hours.

2 Remove and discard bay leaf. Transfer ham to cutting board. Remove skin from ham; cut meat from bones. Return meat to slow cooker. Cover and cook on LOW 15 minutes or until heated through.

TOMATO SOUP WITH DITALINI

• makes 6 servings •

2 cans (28 ounces each) whole plum tomatoes
4 cups vegetable broth
1 medium onion, chopped
1 medium bulb fennel, chopped
2 carrots, chopped
3 tablespoons tomato paste
2 tablespoons olive oil
3 cloves garlic, minced
1 teaspoon dried basil
1 teaspoon salt
¼ teaspoon black pepper
3 cups hot cooked ditalini pasta
Grated Parmesan cheese

1 Spray inside of slow cooker with nonstick cooking spray. Add tomatoes, broth, onion, fennel, carrots, tomato paste, oil, garlic, basil, salt and pepper; stir to blend.

2 Cover and cook on LOW 7 to 8 hours or on HIGH 3 to 4 hours. Stir in pasta. Garnish with cheese.

HEARTY VEGETABLE AND POTATO CHOWDER

• makes 4 servings •

- 2 cups vegetable broth
- 1 can (10½ ounces) cream of mushroom soup
- 1 package (10 ounces) frozen mixed vegetables (corn, carrots, peas and green beans)
- 2 medium russet potatoes (about 1 pound), cut into ½-inch cubes
- 2 to 3 teaspoons minced garlic
- 1½ teaspoons dried thyme
- ½ teaspoon black pepper

1. Spray inside of slow cooker with nonstick cooking spray. Combine broth, soup, mixed vegetables, potatoes, garlic, thyme and pepper in slow cooker; stir to blend.
2. Cover and cook on LOW 7 to 8 hours or on HIGH 3 to 4 hours. Stir to blend.

SAUSAGE AND VEGETABLE SOUP

• makes 6 to 8 servings •

- 2 cups diced potatoes
- 1 can (about 15 ounces) black beans, rinsed and drained
- 1 can (about 14 ounces) diced tomatoes
- 1 can (10½ ounces) cream of mushroom soup
- ½ pound smoked turkey sausage, cut into ½-inch slices
- 1 medium onion, chopped
- 1 medium red bell pepper, chopped
- ¼ cup water
- 2 teaspoons prepared horseradish
- 2 teaspoons honey
- 1 teaspoon dried basil
- Salt and black pepper

1 Combine potatoes, beans, tomatoes, soup, sausage, onion, pepper, water, horseradish, honey and basil in slow cooker; stir to blend.

2 Cover and cook on LOW 7 to 8 hours. Season to taste with salt and black pepper.

HEARTY CHILI MAC

• makes 4 servings •

1 pound ground beef
1 can (about 14 ounces) diced tomatoes, drained
1 cup chopped onion
1 tablespoon chili powder
1 clove garlic, minced
½ teaspoon salt
½ teaspoon ground cumin
½ teaspoon dried oregano
¼ teaspoon red pepper flakes
¼ teaspoon black pepper
2 cups cooked elbow macaroni

1. Brown beef in large nonstick skillet over medium-high heat 6 to 8 minutes, stirring to break up meat. Drain fat. Transfer to slow cooker.
2. Add tomatoes, onion, chili powder, garlic, salt, cumin, oregano, red pepper flakes and black pepper to slow cooker; mix well. Cover and cook on LOW 4 hours.
3. Stir in macaroni. Cover and cook on LOW 1 hour or until macaroni is tender.

CURRIED SWEET POTATO AND CARROT SOUP

• makes 8 servings •

- 2 sweet potatoes, peeled and cut into ¾-inch cubes (about 5 cups)
- 2 cups baby carrots
- 1 onion, chopped
- 2 teaspoons curry powder
- ½ teaspoon salt
- ½ teaspoon black pepper
- ½ teaspoon ground cinnamon
- ¼ teaspoon ground ginger
- 4 cups vegetable broth
- ¾ cup half-and-half
- 1 tablespoon maple syrup
- Candied ginger (optional)

1 Place sweet potatoes, carrots, onion, curry powder, salt, pepper, cinnamon and ground ginger in slow cooker. Stir in broth. Cover and cook on LOW 7 to 8 hours.

2 Working in batches, process soup in blender or food processor until smooth. Return to slow cooker. (Or use immersion blender.) Add half-and-half and maple syrup. Cover and cook on HIGH 15 minutes or until heated through. Garnish with candied ginger.

THREE-BEAN TURKEY CHILI

• makes 6 to 8 servings •

1 pound ground turkey
1 onion, chopped
3 cloves garlic, minced
2 tablespoons chili powder
1 teaspoon salt
1 teaspoon ground cumin
1 teaspoon dried oregano
1 can (28 ounces) diced tomatoes
1 can (about 15 ounces) chickpeas, rinsed and drained
1 can about (15 ounces) kidney beans, rinsed and drained
1 can about (15 ounces) black beans, rinsed and drained
1 can (8 ounces) tomato sauce
1 can (4 ounces) diced mild green chiles

1 Cook turkey in large skillet over medium-high heat 6 to 8 minutes or until no longer pink, stirring to break up meat. Add onion and garlic; cook and stir 5 minutes or until onion is softened. Stir in chili powder, salt, cumin and oregano.

2 Transfer turkey mixture to slow cooker. Stir in tomatoes, beans, tomato sauce and chiles. Cover and cook on HIGH 6 to 8 hours.

MEDITERRANEAN BEAN SOUP WITH ORZO

• makes 4 servings •

- 2 cans (about 14 ounces each) vegetable broth
- 1 can (about 14 ounces) Italian-style diced tomatoes
- 1 package (10 ounces) frozen mixed carrots and peas
- ½ cup uncooked orzo pasta
- 2 teaspoons dried oregano
- ½ teaspoon salt
- 1 can (about 15 ounces) chickpeas, rinsed and drained
- Black pepper
- ½ cup crumbled feta cheese

1 Spray inside of slow cooker with nonstick cooking spray. Combine broth, tomatoes, carrots and peas, pasta, oregano and salt in slow cooker.

2 Cover and cook on LOW 5 to 6 hours or on HIGH 2 to 3 hours. Stir in chickpeas. Cover and cook on HIGH 10 minutes or until heated through. Season to taste with pepper. Top each serving with cheese.

VEGETABLE MEDLEY SOUP

• makes 8 servings •

- 3 cans (about 14 ounces each) vegetable broth
- 3 sweet potatoes, peeled and chopped
- 3 zucchini, chopped
- 2 cups chopped broccoli
- 2 yellow potatoes, peeled and shredded
- 1 onion, chopped
- 1 stalk celery, finely chopped
- 1 teaspoon black pepper
- ¼ cup (½ stick) butter, melted
- 2 cups half-and-half or milk
- 2 teaspoons salt
- 1 teaspoon ground cumin

1. Combine broth, sweet potatoes, zucchini, broccoli, potatoes, onion, celery, pepper and butter in slow cooker. Cover and cook on LOW 8 to 10 hours or on HIGH 4 to 5 hours.
2. Add half-and-half, salt and cumin. Cover and cook 30 minutes to 1 hour or until heated through.

CHICKEN ENCHILADA STEW

• makes 4 servings •

- 1 can (about 14 ounces) diced tomatoes with green chiles
- 1 can (10 ounces) enchilada sauce
- 1 cup frozen or canned corn
- ¼ teaspoon ground cumin
- ¼ teaspoon black pepper
- 1½ pounds boneless skinless chicken thighs, cut into bite-size pieces
- 2 tablespoons minced fresh cilantro
- ½ cup (2 ounces) shredded pepper Jack or Monterey Jack cheese
- Sliced green onions (optional)

1 Combine tomatoes, enchilada sauce, corn, cumin and pepper in slow cooker. Add chicken; mix well to combine. Cover and cook on LOW 6 to 7 hours.

2 Stir in cilantro. Top each serving with cheese and green onions, if desired.

SUPER SIMPLE CHILI

• makes 8 servings •

2 pounds ground beef

3 cans (about 15 ounces each) chili beans in mild or spicy sauce, undrained

4 cans (8 ounces each) tomato sauce

Shredded Cheddar cheese

Sliced green onions

1 Brown beef in large skillet over medium-high heat 6 to 8 minutes, stirring to break up meat. Drain fat. Combine beef, beans and tomato sauce in slow cooker; mix well.

2 Cover and cook on LOW 6 to 8 hours. Top each serving with cheese and green onions.

Main Meats & Poultry

CHICKEN CACCIATORE

• makes 6 to 8 servings •

- ¼ cup vegetable oil
- 2½ to 3 pounds chicken tenders, cut into bite-size pieces
- 1 can (28 ounces) crushed Italian-style tomatoes
- 2 cans (8 ounces each) tomato sauce
- 1 onion, chopped
- 1 can (4 ounces) sliced mushrooms, drained
- 2 cloves garlic, minced
- 1 teaspoon salt
- 1 teaspoon dried oregano
- ½ teaspoon dried thyme
- ½ teaspoon black pepper
- 1 package (16 ounces) uncooked spaghetti

1. Heat oil in large skillet over medium-low heat. Add chicken; cook until browned on all sides.
2. Transfer chicken to slow cooker. Add tomatoes, tomato sauce, onion, mushrooms, garlic, salt, oregano, thyme and pepper. Cover and cook on LOW 6 to 8 hours.
3. Cook pasta in large saucepan of salted boiling water according to package directions for al dente; drain. Serve chicken and sauce over spaghetti.

SOUTHWEST-STYLE MEAT LOAF

• makes 6 servings •

- 1½ pounds ground beef
- 2 eggs
- 1 small onion, chopped
- ½ medium green bell pepper, chopped
- ½ cup plain dry bread crumbs
- ¾ cup chunky salsa, divided
- 1½ teaspoons ground cumin
- ¾ cup (3 ounces) shredded Mexican cheese blend
- ¾ teaspoon salt
- ¼ teaspoon black pepper

1 Combine beef, eggs, onion, bell pepper, bread crumbs, ¼ cup salsa, cumin, cheese, salt and black pepper in large bowl; mix well. Shape into 9×5-inch loaf.

2 Fold two long pieces of foil in half lengthwise. (Each should be about 24 inches long.) Crisscross pieces on work surface; spray with nonstick cooking spray. Place meat loaf on top of foil. Use ends of foil as handles to gently lower meat loaf into slow cooker, letting ends hang over the top. Top meat loaf with remaining ½ cup salsa.

3 Cover and cook on LOW 7 to 8 hours or on HIGH 3 to 4 hours or until meat loaf is firm and cooked through. Remove meat loaf to large cutting board; let stand 5 minutes before slicing.

BRAISED TURKEY WITH LEMON-ARTICHOKE SAUCE

• makes 6 servings •

- 2 bone-in skin-on turkey breast halves (about 2 pounds each)
- Salt and black pepper
- ½ cup all-purpose flour
- 4 teaspoons vegetable oil, divided
- 4 shallots, thinly sliced
- ½ cup dry sherry
- 1 lemon, cut into ¼-inch-thick slices
- 2 tablespoons capers, rinsed and drained
- 4 sprigs fresh thyme
- 1½ cups chicken broth
- 1 package (16 ounces) uncooked egg noodles
- 2 cans (about 14 ounces each) artichoke hearts, drained
- 2 tablespoons finely chopped parsley

1 Season both sides of turkey breasts liberally with salt and pepper. Dredge in flour, shaking off excess. Heat oil in large skillet over medium-high heat. Cook turkey in batches until browned on all sides. Transfer to slow cooker.

2 Reduce heat to medium. Add shallots to skillet; cook and stir 4 minutes or until just beginning to brown. Add sherry; stir to scrape up browned bits. Pour over turkey. Add lemon slices, capers, thyme sprigs, 2 teaspoons salt and ¼ teaspoon pepper. Pour in broth. Cover and cook on LOW 6 hours or until turkey breasts are tender and nearly falling off the bone.

3 Remove turkey breasts; set aside to cool 10 minutes. Remove and discard skin and bones.

4 Cook noodles in large saucepan of salted boiling water according to package directions for al dente; drain.

5 Remove thyme from cooking liquid; discard. Skim fat from sauce. Stir in artichoke hearts and chopped parsley. Season to taste with salt and pepper. Slice turkey; serve on noodles with sauce.

SPICY SAUSAGE BOLOGNESE SAUCE

• makes 6 servings •

1 pound ground beef
1 pound hot Italian sausage, casings removed
1 tablespoon olive oil
4 ounces pancetta or bacon, diced
1 onion, finely diced
2 carrots, finely diced
1 stalk celery, finely diced
½ teaspoon salt
½ teaspoon black pepper
3 tablespoons tomato paste
1 tablespoon minced garlic
2 cans (28 ounces each) diced tomatoes, drained
¾ cup whole milk
¾ cup dry red wine
1 package (16 ounces) uncooked spaghetti
Grated Parmesan cheese (optional)

1 Brown ground beef and Italian sausage 6 to 8 minutes in large skillet over medium-high heat, stirring to break up meat. Transfer to slow cooker.

2 Add oil to skillet; heat over medium heat. Add pancetta; cook until crisp and brown, stirring occasionally. Transfer to slow cooker.

3 Add onion, carrots, celery, salt and pepper to skillet; cook and stir 5 minutes or until vegetables are softened. Add tomato paste and garlic; cook and stir 1 minute. Transfer to slow cooker. Stir in tomatoes, milk and wine. Cover and cook on LOW 6 hours.

4 Cook pasta in large saucepan of salted boiling water according to package directions for al dente; drain. Serve sauce on spaghetti; top with cheese.

ITALIAN BRAISED SHORT RIBS

• makes 4 to 6 servings •

- 3 pounds beef short ribs, trimmed of excess fat
- Salt and black pepper
- 1 to 2 tablespoons vegetable oil
- 2 large onions, sliced
- 2 packages (8 ounces each) cremini mushrooms, quartered
- 2 cups dry red wine
- 2 cups beef broth
- 2 cloves garlic, minced
- 2 teaspoons Italian seasoning
- Mashed potatoes or polenta

1. Spray inside of slow cooker with nonstick cooking spray. Season short ribs with salt and pepper. Heat 1 tablespoon oil in large skillet over medium-high heat. Working in batches, brown short ribs on all sides, adding additional oil as needed. Remove to slow cooker.
2. Add onions to skillet; cook and stir 3 to 5 minutes or until translucent. Stir in mushrooms, wine, broth, garlic and Italian seasoning; bring to a simmer. Cook 3 minutes, stirring occasionally. Pour over short ribs in slow cooker.
3. Cover and cook on LOW 10 to 12 hours or on HIGH 6 to 8 hours or until meat is tender. Season to taste with salt and pepper. Remove short ribs and mushrooms to serving plate. Strain cooking liquid. Serve ribs, vegetables and sauce with mashed potatoes.

APPLE-CHERRY GLAZED PORK CHOPS

• makes 4 servings •

- ½ teaspoon dried thyme
- ¼ teaspoon salt
- ¼ teaspoon black pepper
- 4 boneless pork loin chops (3 ounces each)
- 1 tablespoon vegetable oil
- 1⅓ cups apple juice
- 1 small apple, sliced
- ¼ cup sliced green onions
- ¼ cup dried tart cherries
- 2 tablespoons water
- 2 teaspoons cornstarch

1 Combine thyme, salt and pepper in small bowl. Rub onto both sides of pork chops. Heat oil in large skillet over medium-high heat. Add pork; cook 5 to 7 minutes or until browned on both sides. Place pork in slow cooker.

2 Add apple juice, apple slices, green onion and cherries to same skillet; cook 2 to 3 minutes or until apple and onion are tender. Pour into slow cooker. Cover and cook on LOW 3½ to 4 hours.

3 Remove pork chops to large serving platter; cover to keep warm. Stir water into cornstarch in small bowl; whisk into slow cooker. Cover and cook on HIGH 10 minutes or until thickened. To serve, spoon fruit and cooking liquid over pork chops.

BRISKET WITH BACON, BLUE CHEESE AND ONIONS

• makes 10 servings •

2 large sweet onions, sliced into ½-inch rounds

6 slices bacon

1 flat-cut boneless beef brisket (about 3½ pounds)

Salt and ground black pepper

2 cans (10½ ounces each) beef consommé

1 teaspoon cracked black peppercorns

¾ cup crumbled blue cheese

1 Spray inside of slow cooker with nonstick cooking spray. Spread onion slices in bottom of slow cooker.

2 Heat large skillet over medium-high heat. Add bacon; cook until chewy, not crisp. Reserve drippings in skillet. Drain on paper towel-lined plate. Chop bacon.

3 Season brisket all over with salt and ground pepper. Heat same skillet with bacon drippings over medium-high heat. Add brisket; cook until browned on both sides. Transfer beef to slow cooker. Add consommé; sprinkle with peppercorns and half of bacon. Cover and cook on HIGH 5 to 7 hours.

4 Remove brisket to large cutting board; cover with foil. Let stand 10 to 15 minutes. Slice against the grain into ¾-inch slices. Serve brisket topped with onions, blue cheese and remaining bacon. Season cooking liquid with additional salt and ground pepper; drizzle over brisket.

SWEDISH MEATBALLS

• makes 4 to 6 servings •

- 1½ pounds meatloaf mix*
- ¼ cup plain dry or panko bread crumbs
- 1 egg
- 1 teaspoon salt
- 1 teaspoon onion powder
- 1 teaspoon black pepper
- ¼ teaspoon ground allspice
- 1 cup beef broth
- 2 tablespoons Worcestershire sauce
- 2 tablespoons butter, melted
- 2 tablespoons all-purpose flour
- ¼ cup sour cream
- 1 tablespoon red currant jelly or cranberry sauce
- 1 package (16 ounces) uncooked egg noodles
- Chopped fresh parsley (optional)

**Or substitute ¾ pound ground beef and ¾ pound ground pork.*

1 Combine meatloaf mix, bread crumbs, egg, salt, onion powder, pepper and allspice in large bowl; mix gently but thoroughly. Shape mixture into 24 (1-inch) balls. Refrigerate 1 hour.

2 Combine broth and Worcestershire sauce in slow cooker; add meatballs. Cover and cook on HIGH 5 hours.

3 Transfer meatballs to medium bowl using slotted spoon. Combine butter and flour in small bowl. Whisk half of butter mixture at a time into slow cooker until well blended. Combine sour cream and jelly in small bowl. Whisk half of jelly mixture at a time into slow cooker.

4 Cover and cook on HIGH 30 minutes or until sauce is thickened. Return meatballs to slow cooker; stir to coat.

5 Cook noodles in large saucepan of salted boiling water according to package directions for all dente; drain. Serve meatballs and sauce over noodles; garnish with parsley.

CHICKEN AZTECA

• makes 4 servings •

- 2 cups frozen corn
- 1 can (about 15 ounces) black beans, rinsed and drained
- 1 cup chunky salsa, divided
- 1 clove garlic, minced
- ½ teaspoon ground cumin
- 4 boneless skinless chicken breasts (6 to 8 ounces each)
- 1 package (8 ounces) cream cheese, cubed
- 1 cup uncooked rice, cooked according to package directions
- Shredded Cheddar cheese

1 Combine corn, beans, ½ cup salsa, garlic and cumin in slow cooker. Arrange chicken breasts over top; pour remaining ½ cup salsa over chicken. Cover and cook on HIGH 2 to 3 hours or on LOW 4 to 6 hours or until chicken is tender.

2 Remove chicken to cutting board; cut into bite-size pieces. Return chicken to slow cooker. Add cream cheese. Cook on HIGH until cream cheese melts and blends into sauce, stirring occasionally. Serve chicken and sauce over rice. Top with Cheddar cheese.

LEMON-THYME BEEF WITH BEANS

• makes 6 to 8 servings •

- 3 pounds beef stew meat (1-inch cubes)
- 1 teaspoon salt
- 1 teaspoon grated lemon peel
- 1 teaspoon dried thyme
- 1 teaspoon black pepper
- 2 cans (about 15 ounces each) white or pinto beans, rinsed and drained
- 1 can (about 15 ounces) red kidney beans, rinsed and drained
- 1 medium onion, chopped
- 2 cloves garlic, minced
- 1 cup beef broth
- Chopped fresh parsley

1 Place beef in slow cooker; sprinkle with salt, lemon peel, thyme and pepper. Top with beans, onions and garlic; pour broth over top. Cover and cook on LOW 8 to 9 hours or until beef is tender.

2 Taste and adjust seasonings. Serve beef on top of beans. Garnish with parsley.

PORK TENDERLOIN WITH THYME AND WHITE BEANS

• makes 10 to 12 servings •

- 2 to 3 pork tenderloins (2 to 3 pounds) *or* 1 boneless pork top loin roast (3 to 4 pounds)
- 1 head garlic, peeled and separated into individual cloves
- Salt and black pepper
- 2 cups dried navy beans, rinsed, sorted and soaked overnight
- 1 cup red wine
- ¾ cup white wine
- ¼ cup hot water
- 2 tablespoons dried thyme
- 2 teaspoons dried oregano
- 1 teaspoon chopped garlic
- 1 teaspoon baking soda
- 2 yellow onions, quartered
- 1 leek, cut into ⅛-inch-thick slices
- 1 tablespoon olive oil
- 1 tablespoon butter, melted

1. With paring knife, poke holes about 1 inch deep evenly around tenderloins. Place one garlic clove into each hole. Season with salt and black pepper.
2. Drain beans; place in slow cooker. Add wine, water, thyme, oregano, chopped garlic and baking soda; mix well. Top with onions, leek and pork. Drizzle oil and butter over pork.
3. Cover and cook on LOW for 6 to 8 hours or until beans are tender and pork is cooked through. Transfer pork to cutting board; let stand 10 minutes. Slice pork; serve over beans.

BEEF BOURGUIGNON

• makes 10 servings •

- 3 pounds beef stew meat (1-inch cubes)
- ½ cup all-purpose flour
- 1 tablespoon salt
- ½ teaspoon black pepper
- 4 slices bacon, chopped
- 2 medium carrots, diced
- 8 small unpeeled red potatoes, cut into quarters
- 8 cremini mushrooms, sliced
- 20 pearl onions
- 3 cloves garlic, minced
- 1 bay leaf
- 1 teaspoon dried marjoram
- ½ teaspoon dried thyme
- 2½ cups beef broth

1. Place beef in large bowl. Add flour, salt and pepper; toss until beef is completely coated with flour. Heat large skillet over medium heat. Add bacon; cook and stir until chewy but not crisp. Add beef; cook until browned on all sides.

2. Layer carrots, potatoes, mushrooms, onions, garlic, bay leaf, marjoram and thyme in slow cooker. Top with beef mixture; pour in broth.

3. Cover and cook on LOW 8 to 9 hours or until beef is tender. Remove and discard bay leaf.

TURKEY ROPA VIEJA

• makes 4 servings •

- 12 ounces turkey tenderloin (2 large or 3 small) or boneless skinless chicken thighs
- 1 can (8 ounces) tomato sauce
- 2 medium tomatoes, chopped
- 1 onion, thinly sliced
- 1 green bell pepper, chopped
- 4 pimiento-stuffed green olives, sliced
- 1 clove garlic, minced
- 1 teaspoon salt
- ¾ teaspoon ground cumin
- ½ teaspoon dried oregano
- ⅛ teaspoon black pepper
- 2 teaspoons lemon juice
- 1 cup cooked brown rice (optional)
- 1 can (about 15 ounces) black beans, rinsed and drained (optional)

1 Place turkey in slow cooker. Add tomato sauce, tomatoes, onion, bell pepper, olives, garlic, salt, cumin, oregano and black pepper. Cover and cook on LOW 6 to 7 hours.

2 Shred turkey using two forks. Stir in lemon juice. Serve with rice and black beans, if desired.

ASIAN BEEF WITH BROCCOLI

• makes 4 to 6 servings •

- 1½ pounds boneless beef chuck steak (about 1½ inches thick) thinly sliced*
- 1 can (10½ ounces) beef consommé
- ½ cup oyster sauce
- 2 tablespoons cornstarch
- 1 bag (16 ounces) fresh broccoli florets
- 1 cup uncooked rice, cooked according to package directions
- Sesame seeds (optional)

**To make slicing steak easier, place in freezer for 30 minutes before slicing.*

1 Place steak in slow cooker. Pour in consommé and oyster sauce. Cover and cook on LOW 6 to 8 hours or on HIGH 3 hours.

2 Turn slow cooker to HIGH. Stir 2 tablespoons cooking liquid into cornstarch in small bowl until smooth. Add to slow cooker; stir until blended. Cook, uncovered, 15 minutes or until thickened.

3 Meanwhile, cook broccoli in large saucepan of salted boiling water 4 minutes or until crisp-tender. Stir broccoli into slow cooker. Serve over rice; garnish with sesame seeds.

CREAMY SLOW COOKER PORK CHOPS

• makes 4 to 6 servings •

- 2 cans (10½ ounces each) cream of mushroom soup
- ½ cup milk
- 3 ounces cream cheese, softened
- ¼ cup sour cream
- 4 to 6 pork loin chops, cut ¾-inch thick
- Salt and black pepper
- 2 tablespoons vegetable oil
- 1 jar (2½ ounces) sliced dried beef

1 Stir soup, milk, cream cheese and sour cream in medium bowl until smooth. Season pork all over with salt and pepper. Heat oil in large skillet over medium-high heat. Working in batches if necessary, brown both sides of pork.

2 Spray inside of slow cooker with nonstick cooking spray. Place half of pork chops in slow cooker. Top with 4 slices dried beef. Pour half of sauce mixture over pork. Repeat with remaining pork, dried beef and sauce. Cover and cook on LOW 8 to 9 hours.

SLOW COOKER CHICKEN AND RICE

• makes 4 servings •

- 3 cans (10½ ounces each) cream of chicken soup
- 2 cups uncooked instant rice
- 1 cup water
- 1 pound boneless skinless chicken breasts, cut into 1-inch pieces
- ½ teaspoon salt
- ¼ teaspoon paprika
- ¼ teaspoon black pepper
- ½ cup diced celery

1 Combine soup, rice and water in slow cooker. Add chicken; sprinkle with salt, paprika and pepper. Sprinkle celery over chicken.

2 Cover and cook on LOW 6 to 8 hours or on HIGH 3 to 4 hours.

Vegetarian Entrées

ZITI RATATOUILLE

• makes 6 to 8 servings •

- 1 large eggplant, peeled and cut into ½-inch cubes (about 1 pound)
- 2 medium zucchini, cut into ½-inch cubes
- 1 green or red bell pepper, cut into ½-inch pieces
- 1 onion, chopped
- 4 cloves garlic, minced
- 1 jar (24 to 26 ounces) marinara sauce
- 2 cans (about 14 ounces each) diced tomatoes with garlic and onions
- 8 ounces uncooked ziti pasta
- 1 can (6 ounces) pitted black olives, drained
- 1 teaspoon salt
- ½ teaspoon black pepper
- Lemon juice (optional)
- Shaved Parmesan cheese (optional)

1 Layer eggplant, zucchini, bell pepper, onion, garlic, marinara sauce and tomatoes in slow cooker. Cover and cook on LOW 4½ hours.

2 Stir in pasta, olives, salt and pepper. Cover and cook on LOW 25 minutes or until pasta is tender. Drizzle with lemon juice and sprinkle with Parmesan cheese, if desired.

CHEESE AND SPINACH LASAGNA

• makes 6 servings •

1 container (15 ounces) ricotta cheese

1 package (10 ounces) frozen chopped spinach, thawed and squeezed dry

2 cups (8 ounces) shredded mozzarella cheese, divided

1 egg

½ cup grated Parmesan cheese, divided

¼ teaspoon salt

1 jar (24 to 26 ounces) pasta sauce

½ cup water

6 uncooked lasagna noodles

1 Combine ricotta cheese, spinach, 1½ cups mozzarella cheese, egg, ¼ cup Parmesan cheese and salt in large bowl; mix well. Mix pasta sauce and water in another large bowl.

2 Spray inside of slow cooker with nonstick cooking spray. Spread 1 cup sauce mixture into slow cooker. Layer two noodles over sauce, breaking to fit. Spoon ½ cup sauce mixture over noodles. Spread half of ricotta mixture over pasta sauce. Top with two noodles and remaining ricotta mixture. Top with remaining two noodles and remaining pasta sauce.

3 Cover and cook on LOW 4 to 6 hours or until liquid is absorbed and noodles are tender. Sprinkle remaining ½ cup mozzarella cheese and ¼ cup Parmesan cheese over top; cover and let stand 5 minutes or until cheese is melted.

EGGPLANT PARMESAN

• makes 4 servings •

- ¼ cup all-purpose flour
- 1 teaspoon dried oregano
- 1 teaspoon dried basil
- ½ teaspoon salt
- 1 egg
- 2 teaspoons cold water
- 1 large eggplant (about 1 pound), ends trimmed, peeled and cut crosswise into 8 slices
- 2 tablespoons olive oil
- 2¼ cups spicy marinara pasta sauce
- ½ cup panko bread crumbs
- 1½ cups (6 ounces) shredded Italian cheese blend or mozzarella cheese
- Chopped fresh basil (optional)

1 Combine flour, oregano, dried basil and salt in shallow dish. Beat egg with water in another shallow dish. Dip each slice of eggplant in egg mixture, letting excess drip back into dish. Dredge in flour mixture, coating both sides lightly.

2 Heat oil in large skillet over medium heat. Working in batches, cook eggplant 3 minutes per side or until lightly browned.

3 Spray inside of slow cooker with nonstick cooking spray. Layer ¾ cup pasta sauce in bottom of slow cooker. Arrange four eggplant slices over sauce, overlapping if necessary. Top with ¼ cup panko and ½ cup cheese. Repeat layering with ¾ cup pasta sauce, four slices eggplant, ¼ cup panko and ½ cup cheese. Spoon remaining pasta sauce over cheese. Cover and cook on LOW 4 to 5 hours or on HIGH 2 to 2½ hours.

4 Sprinkle remaining ½ cup cheese over top. Cover and let stand 5 minutes or until cheese is melted. Garnish with fresh basil.

STUFFED MANICOTTI

• makes 5 servings •

1 container (15 ounces) ricotta cheese

1½ cups (6 ounces) shredded Italian cheese blend, divided

1 egg

¼ teaspoon ground nutmeg

10 uncooked manicotti shells

2 cans (about 14 ounces each) diced tomatoes

1 cup spicy marinara or tomato-basil pasta sauce

Chopped fresh basil or parsley (optional)

1 Combine ricotta cheese, 1 cup Italian cheese, egg and nutmeg in medium bowl; mix well. Spoon mixture into large resealable food storage bag; cut off small corner. Pipe cheese mixture into uncooked manicotti shells.

2 Spray inside of slow cooker with nonstick cooking spray. Combine tomatoes and pasta sauce in large bowl; stir until blended. Spoon 1½ cups sauce mixture into slow cooker. Arrange half of manicotti shells in sauce. Repeat layering with 1½ cups sauce, remaining shells and remaining sauce. Cover and cook on LOW 2½ to 3 hours.

3 Sprinkle remaining ½ cup Italian cheese over top. Turn slow cooker to HIGH. Cover and cook on HIGH 10 to 15 minutes or until cheese is melted. Garnish with basil.

VEGETARIAN PAELLA

• makes 6 servings •

- 2 tablespoons olive oil
- 1 medium onion, chopped
- 1 medium red bell pepper, chopped
- 2 cloves garlic, minced
- 1½ cups uncooked converted rice
- 2 cans (about 14 ounces each) vegetable broth
- ½ cup dry white wine
- ½ teaspoon crushed saffron threads, smoked paprika or ground turmeric
- 1 teaspoon salt
- ¼ teaspoon red pepper flakes
- 1 can (about 15 ounces) chickpeas
- 1 package (11 ounces) frozen artichoke hearts, thawed
- ½ cup frozen peas, thawed

1 Heat oil in medium skillet over medium heat. Add onion, bell pepper and garlic; cook and stir 5 minutes or until onion is softened. Transfer to slow cooker. Add rice, broth, wine, saffron, salt and red pepper flakes; mix well. Cover and cook on LOW 3 hours.

2 Add chickpeas, artichokes and peas to slow cooker; do not stir. Cover and cook on LOW about 30 minutes or until rice is tender and liquid is absorbed. Stir before serving.

BLACK BEAN AND MUSHROOM CHILAQUILES

• makes 6 servings •

- 2 tablespoons olive oil
- 1 medium onion, chopped
- 1 medium green bell pepper, chopped
- 1 jalapeño or serrano pepper, seeded and minced
- 2 cans (about 15 ounces each) black beans, rinsed and drained
- 1 can (about 14 ounces) diced tomatoes
- 1 package (8 ounces) whole mushrooms, cut into quarters
- 1½ teaspoons ground cumin
- 1½ teaspoons dried oregano
- ½ teaspoon salt
- 1 cup (4 ounces) shredded sharp Cheddar cheese, plus additional for garnish
- 6 cups tortilla chips, coarsely crushed

1 Heat oil in medium skillet over medium heat. Add onion, bell pepper and minced jalapeño; cook and stir 5 minutes or until onion is softened. Transfer to slow cooker. Add beans, tomatoes, mushrooms, cumin, oregano and salt. Cover and cook on LOW 6 hours or on HIGH 3 hours.

2 Sprinkle 1 cup cheese over top. Cover and let stand until cheese is melted. Stir to combine. Place tortilla chips in serving bowls. Top with black bean mixture and sprinkle with additional cheese.

LAYERED MEXICAN-STYLE CASSEROLE

• makes 6 servings •

- 2 cans (about 15 ounces each) hominy, drained*
- 1 can (about 15 ounces) black beans, rinsed and drained
- 1 can (about 14 ounces) diced tomatoes with garlic, basil and oregano
- 1 cup thick and chunky salsa
- 1 can (6 ounces) tomato paste
- ½ teaspoon ground cumin
- 3 (9-inch) flour tortillas
- 2 cups (8 ounces) shredded Monterey Jack cheese
- ¼ cup sliced black olives

**Hominy is corn that has been treated to remove the germ and hull. It can be found with the canned vegetables or beans in most supermarkets.*

1 Prepare foil handles (see below). Spray inside of slow cooker with nonstick cooking spray.

2 Combine hominy, beans, tomatoes, salsa, tomato paste and cumin in large bowl.

3 Press one tortilla in bottom of slow cooker. (Edges of tortilla may turn up slightly.) Top with one third of hominy mixture and one third of cheese. Repeat layers. Press remaining tortilla on top. Top with remaining hominy mixture. Refrigerate remaining cheese.

4 Cover and cook on LOW 6 to 8 hours. Sprinkle with remaining cheese and olives. Cover and let stand 5 minutes. Pull out tortilla stack with foil handles.

FOIL HANDLES: Tear off three (18×2-inch) strips of heavy-duty foil or use regular foil folded to double thickness. Crisscross foil strips in spoke design and place into slow cooker to make lifting of tortilla stack easier.

BLACK BEAN, ZUCCHINI AND CORN ENCHILADAS

• makes 6 servings •

- 1 tablespoon vegetable oil
- 1 medium onion, chopped
- 2 medium zucchini, diced
- 2 cups corn
- 1 red bell pepper, chopped
- 1 teaspoon minced garlic
- ½ teaspoon salt
- ½ teaspoon ground cumin
- ¼ teaspoon ground coriander
- 1 can (about 15 ounces) black beans, rinsed and drained
- 3 cups salsa verde
- 12 (6-inch) corn tortillas
- 2½ cups (10 ounces) shredded Monterey Jack cheese
- 2 tablespoons chopped fresh cilantro

1 Heat oil in large skillet over medium heat. Add onion; cook and stir 5 minutes or until softened. Add zucchini, corn and bell pepper; cook and stir 2 minutes. Add garlic, salt, cumin and coriander; cook and stir 1 minute. Stir in beans. Remove from heat.

2 Pour 1 cup salsa in bottom of slow cooker. Arrange three tortillas in single layer, cutting tortillas in half as needed to fit. Spread 2 cups vegetable mixture over tortillas; sprinkle with ½ cup cheese. Repeat layering two more times. Layer with remaining three tortillas; top with 2 cups salsa. Sprinkle with remaining 1 cup cheese. Reserve remaining filling for another use.

3 Cover and cook on HIGH 2 hours or until cheese is bubbly and edges are lightly browned. Sprinkle with cilantro. Turn off heat. Let stand, uncovered, 10 minutes before serving.

TOFU TIKKA MASALA

• makes 4 to 6 servings •

- 1 package (14 to 16 ounces) extra firm tofu, cut into 1-inch pieces
- ½ cup whole milk yogurt
- 2 teaspoons salt, divided
- 1 tablespoon plus 1 teaspoon minced garlic, divided
- 2½ teaspoons grated fresh ginger, divided
- 2 tablespoons vegetable oil
- 1 medium onion, chopped
- 2 tablespoons tomato paste
- 1 tablespoon garam masala
- 1 can (28 ounces) crushed tomatoes
- 1 teaspoon sugar
- ½ cup whipping cream
- 3 tablespoons chopped fresh cilantro
- 1 cup uncooked basmati rice, cooked according to package directions

1 Combine tofu, yogurt, 1 teaspoon salt, 1 teaspoon garlic and 1 teaspoon ginger in large bowl; stir to blend. Cover; refrigerate 1 hour or overnight.

2 Heat oil in large skillet over medium heat. Add onion; cook and stir 5 minutes or until softened. Add remaining 1 tablespoon garlic, remaining 1½ teaspoons ginger, tomato paste, remaining 1 teaspoon salt and garam masala; cook and stir 1 minute. Add tomatoes and sugar; bring to a simmer. Pour mixture into slow cooker. Add tofu using slotted spoon; stir to blend.

3 Cover and cook on LOW 8 hours or on HIGH 4 hours. Stir in cream and cilantro. Serve over rice.

SPINACH AND RICOTTA STUFFED SHELLS

• makes 4 to 6 servings •

- 1 package (16 ounces) jumbo pasta shells
- 1 container (15 ounces) ricotta cheese
- 1 package (10 ounces) frozen chopped spinach, thawed and squeezed dry
- ½ cup grated Parmesan cheese
- 1 egg
- 1 clove garlic, minced
- ½ teaspoon salt
- 1 jar (24 to 26 ounces) marinara pasta sauce
- ½ cup (2 ounces) shredded mozzarella cheese
- 1 teaspoon olive oil

1 Cook pasta shells according to package directions until almost tender; drain. Combine ricotta cheese, spinach, Parmesan cheese, egg, garlic and salt in large bowl.

2 Pour ¼ cup marinara sauce in bottom of slow cooker. Spoon 2 tablespoons ricotta mixture into one pasta shell and place in bottom of slow cooker. Repeat with enough additional shells to cover bottom of slow cooker. Top with ¼ cup marinara sauce. Repeat with remaining pasta shells and filling. Top with any remaining marinara sauce and sprinkle with mozzarella cheese. Drizzle with oil.

3 Cover and cook on HIGH 3 to 4 hours or until mozzarella cheese is melted and sauce is hot and bubbly.

Pasta & Grains

GARLIC AND HERB POLENTA

• makes 6 servings •

- 3 tablespoons butter, divided
- 8 cups water
- 2 cups yellow cornmeal
- 2 teaspoons finely minced garlic
- 2 teaspoons salt
- 3 tablespoons chopped fresh herbs such as parsley, chives, thyme or chervil (or a combination)

1 Grease inside of slow cooker with 1 tablespoon butter. Add water, cornmeal, remaining 2 tablespoons butter, garlic and salt; mix well. Cover and cook on LOW 4 hours or on HIGH 3 hours, stirring occasionally.

2 Stir in chopped herbs just before serving.

TIP: Spread leftover polenta into a greased pan and allowed to cool until set. Cut into squares or slices, chill until firm and then grill or fry until golden brown.

PIZZA-STYLE MOSTACCIOLI

• makes 4 servings •

- 1 jar (24 to 26 ounces) marinara sauce or tomato-basil pasta sauce
- ½ cup water
- 2 cups uncooked mostaccioli or penne pasta
- 1 package (8 ounces) sliced mushrooms
- 1 yellow or green bell pepper, finely diced
- ½ cup sliced pepperoni, halved
- 1 teaspoon dried oregano
- ¼ teaspoon red pepper flakes
- 1 cup (4 ounces) shredded pizza cheese blend or Italian cheese blend
- Chopped fresh oregano or parsley (optional)

1. Spray inside of slow cooker with nonstick cooking spray. Combine marinara sauce and water in slow cooker. Stir in pasta, mushrooms, bell pepper, pepperoni, dried oregano and red pepper flakes; mix well. Cover and cook on LOW 4 hours or on HIGH 2 hours, stirring halfway through cooking time.
2. Serve with cheese and garnish with fresh oregano.

SWEET CHILI CHICKEN AND NOODLES

• makes 4 to 6 servings •

- 2 teaspoons olive oil
- 1½ pounds boneless skinless chicken breasts, cut into thin strips
- 1 bottle (about 10 ounces) Asian-style sweet chili sauce
- 3 tablespoons creamy peanut butter
- 3 cloves garlic, minced
- 1 can (about 14 ounces) chicken broth
- 8 ounces uncooked vermicelli noodles
- 1 cup shredded cabbage and carrot mix
- Bean sprouts, chopped fresh cilantro and chopped roasted peanuts (optional)

1 Heat oil in large nonstick skillet over medium-high heat. Working in batches, brown chicken on all sides. Transfer to slow cooker.

2 Combine sweet chili sauce, peanut butter and garlic in small bowl; pour over chicken, stirring to coat. Stir in broth. Cover and cook on LOW 2 hours.

3 Add noodles and cabbage mix. Cover and cook on LOW 30 minutes or until noodles and vegetables are tender. Serve with desired toppings.

SIMMERED RED BEANS WITH RICE

• makes 6 servings •

2 cans (about 15 ounces each) dark red kidney beans, rinsed and drained
1 can (about 14 ounces) diced tomatoes
½ cup chopped celery
½ cup chopped green bell pepper
½ cup chopped green onions
2 cloves garlic, minced
1 to 2 teaspoons hot pepper sauce
1 teaspoon Worcestershire sauce
1 bay leaf
Salt and black pepper
1½ cups uncooked rice, cooked according to package directions

1 Combine beans, tomatoes, celery, bell pepper, green onions, garlic, hot pepper sauce, Worcestershire sauce and bay leaf in slow cooker. Season to taste with salt and pepper. Cover and cook on LOW 4 to 6 hours or on HIGH 2 to 3 hours.

2 Slightly mash mixture in slow cooker with potato masher to thicken. Cover and cook on LOW 30 minutes to 1 hour. Remove and discard bay leaf. Serve beans over rice.

NO-FUSS MACARONI AND CHEESE

• makes 6 to 8 servings •

2 cups uncooked elbow macaroni

4 ounces pasteurized process cheese product, cubed

1 cup (4 ounces) shredded mild Cheddar cheese

½ teaspoon salt

⅛ teaspoon black pepper

1½ cups milk

Combine macaroni, cheeses, salt and pepper in slow cooker. Pour milk over top. Cover and cook on LOW 2 to 3 hours, stirring after 20 to 30 minutes.

NOTE: As with all macaroni and cheese dishes, the cheese sauce thickens and begins to dry out as it sits. If it becomes too dry, stir in a little extra milk. Do not cook longer than 4 hours.

RIGATONI WITH BROCCOLI RABE AND SAUSAGE

• makes 6 servings •

- 2 tablespoons olive oil
- 3 sweet or hot Italian sausage links, casings removed
- 2 cloves garlic, minced
- 1 large bunch broccoli rabe (about 1¼ pounds), rinsed well
- ½ cup chicken broth or water
- ½ teaspoon salt
- ½ teaspoon red pepper flakes
- 1 package (16 ounces) uncooked rigatoni pasta
- Grated Parmesan cheese (optional)

1 Spray inside of slow cooker with nonstick cooking spray.

2 Heat oil in large skillet over medium heat. Add sausage; cook 6 to 8 minutes or until browned, stirring to break up meat. Add garlic; cook and stir 1 minute or until softened and fragrant.

3 Trim any woody parts from bottoms of broccoli rabe stems and discard. Cut broccoli rabe into 1-inch pieces; place in slow cooker. Add sausage. Pour in broth and sprinkle with salt and red pepper flakes. Cover and cook on LOW 4 hours or on HIGH 2 hours.

4 Meanwhile, cook pasta in large saucepan of salted boiling water according to package directions for al dente. Drain and stir into slow cooker. Top each serving with cheese.

CREAMY BARLEY RISOTTO

• makes 4 servings •

- 3 cups vegetable broth
- 1 cup uncooked pearl barley
- 1 large leek, white and light green parts thinly sliced, separated into rings
- 1 cup frozen peas
- 1 tablespoon lemon juice
- 1 teaspoon grated lemon peel, plus additional for garnish
- 2 tablespoons butter, cut into pieces
- Salt and black pepper
- Shaved Parmesan cheese (optional)
- Chopped fresh Italian parsley (optional)

1 Spray inside of slow cooker with nonstick cooking spray. Combine broth, barley and leek in slow cooker. Cover and cook on LOW 4 to 5 hours or on HIGH 2 to 2½ hours or until most liquid is absorbed.

2 Stir in peas, lemon juice and 1 teaspoon lemon peel. Cover and cook on HIGH 10 minutes or until heated through. Stir in butter until melted. Season to taste with salt and pepper. Garnish with Parmesan cheese, parsley and additional lemon peel.

GARDEN PASTA

• makes 4 to 6 servings •

- 1 jar (24 to 26 ounces) puttanesca or spicy tomato basil pasta sauce
- 1 can (about 14 ounces) diced tomatoes
- 1 small head broccoli, cut into florets (about 2 cups)
- 1 small zucchini, chopped (about 2 cups)
- 1 small yellow squash, chopped (about 2 cups)
- ½ cup water
- 1 teaspoon salt
- 1 package (16 ounces) uncooked bowtie pasta
- ½ cup crumbled feta cheese
- ¼ cup chopped fresh basil

1. Spray inside of slow cooker with nonstick cooking spray. Combine pasta sauce, tomatoes, broccoli, zucchini, squash, water and salt in slow cooker. Stir in pasta until well blended.
2. Cover and cook on LOW 3½ to 4½ hours or on HIGH 2 to 2½ hours, stirring halfway through cooking time. Top each serving with cheese and basil.

TURKEY AND MACARONI

• makes 4 to 6 servings •

- 1 teaspoon vegetable oil
- 1½ pounds ground turkey
- 2 cans (10¾ ounces each) condensed tomato soup
- 1 can (16 ounces) corn, drained
- ½ cup chopped onion
- 1 can (4 ounces) sliced mushrooms, drained
- 2 tablespoons ketchup
- 1 tablespoon mustard
- Salt and black pepper
- 2 cups uncooked elbow macaroni

1 Heat oil in large nonstick skillet over medium-high heat. Add turkey; cook 6 to 8 minutes until turkey is no longer pink, stirring to break up meat. Transfer to slow cooker.

2 Add soup, corn, onion, mushrooms, ketchup, mustard, salt and pepper to slow cooker; mix well. Cover and cook on LOW 6 to 8 hours or on HIGH 3 to 4 hours.

3 Cook macaroni in large saucepan of salted boiling water according to package directions for al dente. Drain and stir into slow cooker. Cover and cook on LOW 30 minutes or until pasta is tender.

RISOTTO-STYLE PEPPERED RICE

• makes 4 to 6 servings •

- 1 cup uncooked long grain rice
- 1 green bell pepper, chopped
- 1 red bell pepper, chopped
- 1 cup chopped onion
- ½ teaspoon salt
- ½ teaspoon ground turmeric
- ⅛ teaspoon ground red pepper (optional)
- 1 can (about 14 ounces) vegetable broth
- 1 cup (4 ounces) pepper Jack cheese, cubed
- ½ cup milk
- ¼ cup (½ stick) butter, cubed
- 1 teaspoon salt

1. Place rice, bell peppers, onion, salt, turmeric and ground red pepper, if desired, in slow cooker. Stir in broth. Cover and cook on LOW 4 to 5 hours.
2. Stir in cheese, milk, butter and salt; fluff rice with fork. Cover and cook on LOW 5 minutes or until cheese melts.

VEGGIE MAC AND TUNA

• makes 6 servings •

- 2 cups uncooked elbow macaroni
- 3 tablespoons butter
- 1 onion, chopped
- ½ red bell pepper, chopped
- ½ green bell pepper, chopped
- ¼ cup all-purpose flour
- 1¾ cups milk
- 8 ounces cubed pasteurized process cheese product
- ½ teaspoon dried marjoram leaves
- 1 package (10 ounces) frozen peas
- 1 can (9 ounces) tuna in water, drained

1 Cook macaroni in large saucepan of salted boiling water 2 minutes less than package directs for al dente; drain.

2 Melt butter in medium saucepan over medium heat. Add onion and bell peppers; cook and stir 5 minutes or until tender. Add flour; cook and stir 2 minutes over medium heat. Stir in milk. Bring to a boil; cook until thickened. Remove from heat; stir in cheese product until melted. Stir in marjoram.

3 Combine macaroni, cheese sauce, peas and tuna in slow cooker. Cover and cook on LOW 2½ hours or until bubbly at edge.

CHEESY CHICKEN AND NOODLES

• makes 6 servings •

- 8 ounces uncooked wide egg noodles, cooked and drained
- 3 cups chopped cooked chicken
- 1½ cups cottage cheese
- 1 can (10½ ounces) cream of chicken soup
- 1 cup (4 ounces) shredded Monterey Jack cheese
- ½ cup grated Parmesan cheese
- ½ cup diced onion
- ½ cup diced celery
- ½ cup diced green bell pepper
- ½ cup diced red bell pepper
- ½ cup chicken broth
- 1 can (4 ounces) sliced mushrooms, drained
- 2 tablespoons butter, melted
- ½ teaspoon dried thyme

1 Cook noodles in large saucepan of salted boiling water 3 minutes less than package directs for al dente. Drain and place in slow cooker.

2 Stir in chicken, cottage cheese, soup, Monterey Jack cheese, Parmesan cheese, onion, celery, bell peppers, broth, mushrooms, butter and thyme. Cover and cook on LOW 6 to 8 hours or on HIGH 3 to 4 hours.

FIESTA RICE AND SAUSAGE

• makes 10 to 12 servings •

- 2 pounds spicy Italian sausage, casings removed
- 2 cloves garlic, minced
- 2 teaspoons ground cumin
- 4 cups chopped onions
- 4 green bell peppers, chopped
- 3 jalapeño peppers, seeded and minced
- 4 cups beef broth
- 2 packages (6¼ ounces each) long grain and wild rice mix

1. Brown sausage in large nonstick skillet over medium-high heat 6 to 8 minutes, stirring to break up meat. Drain fat. Add garlic and cumin; cook and stir 30 seconds. Add onions, bell peppers and jalapeño peppers; cook and stir 5 minutes or until onions are tender.
2. Transfer mixture to slow cooker. Stir in broth and rice. Cover and cook on LOW 4 to 6 hours or on HIGH 2 to 3 hours.

HAM AND CHEESE PASTA CASSEROLE

• makes 6 servings •

12 ounces uncooked rigatoni pasta

1 ham steak, cubed

1 container (10 ounces) refrigerated Alfredo sauce

2 cups (8 ounces) shredded mozzarella cheese, divided

2 cups half-and-half, warmed

1 tablespoon cornstarch

1 Cook pasta in large saucepan of salted boiling water 2 minutes less than package directs for al dente. Drain and transfer to slow cooker.

2 Stir in ham, Alfredo sauce and 1 cup cheese. Whisk half-and-half and cornstarch in medium bowl; pour over pasta. Top with remaining cheese. Cover and cook on LOW 3½ to 4 hours or until pasta is tender and sauce is creamy. Stir well before serving.

SOUTH OF THE BORDER MACARONI AND CHEESE

• makes 4 servings •

5 cups cooked rotini pasta
1 can (12 ounces) evaporated milk
8 ounces cubed American cheese
4 ounces cubed sharp Cheddar cheese
1 can (4 ounces) diced mild green chiles, drained
2 teaspoons chili powder
2 medium tomatoes, seeded and chopped
5 green onions, sliced

1 Combine pasta, evaporated milk, American cheese, Cheddar cheese, chiles and chili powder in slow cooker; mix well. Cover and cook on HIGH 2 hours, stirring occasionally.

2 Stir in tomatoes and green onions; cook until heated through.

Sandwiches & Tacos

SHREDDED CHICKEN TACOS

• makes 4 servings •

2 pounds boneless skinless chicken thighs

½ cup mango salsa, plus additional for serving

1 cup shredded lettuce (optional)

8 (6-inch) yellow corn tortillas, warmed

1 Spray inside of slow cooker with nonstick cooking spray. Add chicken and ½ cup salsa. Cover and cook on LOW 4 to 5 hours or on HIGH 2½ to 3 hours.

2 Transfer chicken to large cutting board; shred with two forks. Stir shredded chicken back into slow cooker. Divide chicken and lettuce, if desired, evenly among tortillas. Serve with additional salsa.

BARBECUE BEEF SLIDERS

• makes 6 servings •

1 tablespoon packed brown sugar
1 teaspoon ground cumin
1 teaspoon chili powder
1 teaspoon paprika
½ teaspoon salt
¼ teaspoon ground red pepper
3 pounds beef short ribs
½ cup plus 2 tablespoons barbecue sauce, divided
¼ cup water
12 slider rolls
¾ cup prepared coleslaw
12 bread and butter pickle chips

1 Coat inside of slow cooker with nonstick cooking spray. Combine brown sugar, cumin, chili powder, paprika, salt and ground red pepper in small bowl. Rub all over ribs. Place in slow cooker. Pour in ½ cup barbecue sauce and water; turn to coat ribs. Cover and cook on LOW 7 to 8 hours or on HIGH 4 to 4½ hours or until ribs are very tender and meat shreds easily.

2 Transfer ribs to large bowl. Remove bones; shred meat with two forks, discarding any large pieces of fat. Stir in remaining 2 tablespoons barbecue sauce and 2 tablespoons liquid from slow cooker.

3 Serve ¼ cup beef mixture, 1 tablespoon coleslaw and one pickle chip on each roll.

CHICKEN ENCHILADA ROLL-UPS

• makes 6 servings •

- **1½ pounds boneless skinless chicken breasts**
- **½ cup plus 2 tablespoons all-purpose flour, divided**
- **½ teaspoon salt**
- **2 tablespoons butter**
- **1 cup chicken broth**
- **1 small onion, chopped**
- **¼ to ½ cup canned jalapeño peppers, sliced**
- **½ teaspoon dried oregano**
- **2 tablespoons whipping cream or milk**
- **6 (7- to 8-inch) flour tortillas**
- **6 thin slices American cheese or American cheese with jalapeño peppers**

1 Cut each chicken breast lengthwise into 2 or 3 strips. Combine ½ cup flour and salt in large bowl. Add chicken strips; toss to coat. Melt butter in large skillet over medium heat. Working in batches, brown chicken 2 to 3 minutes per side. Place chicken in slow cooker.

2 Add broth to skillet, stirring to scrape up browned bits from bottom of skillet. Pour broth mixture into slow cooker. Add onion, jalapeño peppers and oregano. Cover and cook on LOW 7 to 8 hours or on HIGH 3 to 4 hours.

3 Stir cream into remaining 2 tablespoons flour in small bowl until smooth. Stir into chicken mixture. Cook, uncovered, on HIGH 15 minutes or until thickened. Spoon chicken mixture onto center of flour tortillas. Top with one cheese slice. Fold up tortillas and serve.

HOISIN BARBECUE CHICKEN SLIDERS

• makes 16 sliders •

- ⅔ cup hoisin sauce
- ⅓ cup barbecue sauce
- 3 tablespoons quick-cooking tapioca
- 1 tablespoon sugar
- 1 tablespoon soy sauce
- ¼ teaspoon red pepper flakes
- 12 boneless skinless chicken thighs (3 to 3½ pounds total)
- ½ medium red onion, finely chopped
- Sliced pickles (optional)
- 16 dinner rolls or Hawaiian sweet rolls, split

1. Combine hoisin sauce, barbecue sauce, tapioca, sugar, soy sauce and red pepper flakes in slow cooker; mix well. Add chicken; stir to coat. Cover and cook on LOW 8 to 9 hours.
2. Transfer chicken to large bowl; coarsely shred with two forks. Stir chicken back into slow cooker; mix well.
3. Serve chicken, sauce, onion and pickles, if desired, on rolls.

HOT CHICKEN BAGUETTES

• makes 6 servings •

1 red bell pepper, cut into chunks
1 to 2 carrots, sliced
½ cup sliced celery
1 small onion, chopped
1 clove garlic, minced
¼ teaspoon dried oregano
¼ teaspoon red pepper flakes
6 boneless skinless chicken thighs or breasts
¼ cup all-purpose flour
1 teaspoon salt
½ teaspoon black pepper
1 tablespoon vegetable oil
1 can (about 14 ounces) chicken broth
6 slices Swiss cheese
6 small French bread baguettes or sub rolls, split and toasted

1 Place bell pepper, carrots, celery, onion, garlic, oregano and red pepper flakes in slow cooker.

2 Trim and discard fat from chicken. Combine flour, salt and pepper in large bowl. Coat chicken with flour mixture. Heat oil in large skillet over medium-high heat. Working in batches, cook chicken about 2 minutes per side or until browned.

3 Place chicken on top of vegetables in slow cooker; add broth. Cover and cook on LOW 5 to 6 hours.

4 Transfer chicken to cutting board; cut into pieces. Serve chicken, vegetables, cheese and sauce from slow cooker on baguettes.

MINI CARNITAS TACOS

• makes 36 mini tacos •

1½ pounds boneless pork loin, cut into 1-inch cubes
1 onion, finely chopped
½ cup chicken broth
1 tablespoon chili powder
2 teaspoons ground cumin
1 teaspoon salt
1 teaspoon dried oregano
½ teaspoon minced canned chipotle pepper in adobo sauce (optional)
½ cup pico de gallo
2 tablespoons chopped fresh cilantro
12 (6-inch) corn tortillas
¾ cup (3 ounces) shredded sharp Cheddar cheese
3 tablespoons sour cream

1 Combine pork, onion, broth, chili powder, cumin, salt, oregano and chipotle pepper, if desired, in slow cooker. Cover and cook on LOW 6 hours or on HIGH 3 hours or until pork is very tender. Pour off excess cooking liquid.

2 Shred pork with two forks; stir in pico de gallo and cilantro.

3 Cut three circles from each tortilla with 2-inch biscuit cutter. Top with pork, cheese and sour cream.

CUBAN PORK SANDWICHES

• makes 8 servings •

- 1 pork loin roast (about 2 pounds)
- ½ cup orange juice
- 2 tablespoons lime juice
- 1 tablespoon minced garlic
- 1½ teaspoons salt
- ½ teaspoon red pepper flakes
- 2 tablespoons yellow mustard
- 8 crusty bread rolls, split in half (6 inches each)
- 8 slices Swiss cheese
- 8 thin ham slices
- 4 small dill pickles, thinly sliced lengthwise

1. Coat inside of slow cooker with cooking spray; add pork loin.
2. Combine orange juice, lime juice, garlic, salt and red pepper flakes in small bowl. Pour over pork. Cover and cook on LOW 7 to 8 hours or on HIGH 3½ to 4 hours. Transfer pork to cutting board and allow to cool. Cut into thin slices.
3. Spread mustard on cut sides of rolls. Divide pork slices among roll bottoms. Top each with cheese slice, ham slice and pickle slices; cover with top of roll.
4. Coat large skillet with cooking spray; heat over medium heat. Working in batches, arrange sandwiches in skillet. Cover with foil and top with dinner plate to press down sandwiches. (If necessary, weigh down with 2 to 3 cans to compress sandwiches lightly.) Heat until bread is toasted and cheese is slightly melted.*

**Or use panini press to heat sandwiches.*

DILLY BEEF SANDWICHES

• makes 6 to 8 servings •

1 boneless beef chuck roast (3 to 4 pounds), trimmed

1 jar (6 ounces) sliced dill pickles, undrained

1 can (about 14 ounces) crushed tomatoes with Italian seasoning

1 medium onion, diced

4 cloves garlic, minced

1 teaspoon mustard seeds

Sandwich rolls, toasted

Optional toppings: lettuce, sliced tomatoes and/or sliced red onions

1 Cut beef into chunks. Place in slow cooker. Pour pickles with juice over beef. Add tomatoes, onion, garlic and mustard seeds. Cover and cook on LOW 8 to 10 hours.

2 Transfer beef to large cutting board; shred with two forks. Return beef to slow cooker; mix well. Serve on rolls with desired toppings.

SHREDDED BEEF FAJITAS

• makes 6 servings •

- 1 beef flank steak (about 1 pound)
- 1 can (about 14 ounces) diced tomatoes with mild green chiles
- 1 cup chopped onion
- ½ medium green bell pepper, cut into ½-inch pieces
- ½ package (about 2 tablespoons) fajita seasoning mix
- 1 clove garlic, minced *or* ¼ teaspoon garlic powder
- 6 (8-inch) flour tortillas
- Optional toppings: cilantro, sour cream, guacamole, shredded Cheddar cheese and/or salsa

1. Cut beef into six portions; place in slow cooker. Combine tomatoes, onion, bell pepper, fajita seasoning mix and garlic in medium bowl. Pour over beef. Cover and cook on LOW 8 to 10 hours or on HIGH 4 to 5 hours.
2. Transfer beef to large cutting board; shred with two forks. Return beef to slow cooker; mix well. Serve beef mixture and desired toppings in tortillas.

MEATBALL GRINDERS

• makes 4 servings •

- 1 can (about 14 ounces) diced tomatoes
- 1 can (8 ounces) tomato sauce
- ¼ cup chopped onion
- 2 tablespoons tomato paste
- 1 teaspoon Italian seasoning
- ½ teaspoon salt, divided
- 1 pound ground chicken
- ½ cup fresh bread crumbs (from one bread slice)
- 1 egg
- 3 tablespoons finely chopped fresh parsley
- 2 cloves garlic, minced
- ⅛ teaspoon black pepper
- 1 tablespoon vegetable oil
- 4 small hard rolls, split
- 2 tablespoons grated Parmesan cheese

1. Combine tomatoes, tomato sauce, onion, tomato paste and Italian seasoning and ¼ teaspoon salt in slow cooker. Cover and cook on LOW 2 hours.

2. Combine chicken, bread crumbs, egg, parsley, garlic, remaining ¼ teaspoon salt and pepper in medium bowl. Shape mixture into 12 to 16 meatballs. Heat oil in large nonstick skillet over medium heat. Add meatballs; cook about 8 to 10 minutes or until well browned on all sides.

3. Place meatballs in sauce in slow cooker. Cover and cook on LOW 1 to 2 hours or until meatballs are no longer pink in centers (165°F). Place 3 to 4 meatballs in each roll. Spoon sauce over meatballs; sprinkle with cheese.

BBQ PULLED CHICKEN SANDWICHES

• makes 4 servings •

1½ pounds boneless skinless chicken thighs
¾ cup barbecue sauce, divided
1 green bell pepper, chopped
1 red bell pepper, chopped
1 onion, sliced
¼ to ½ teaspoon hot pepper sauce
4 Kaiser rolls, split and toasted

1 Combine chicken and ¼ cup barbecue sauce in slow cooker; mix well. Add bell peppers and onion; mix well. Cover and cook on LOW 5 to 6 hours or on HIGH 2 to 3 hours.

2 Transfer chicken to medium bowl; shred with two forks. Drain pepper mixture; add to bowl with chicken. Add remaining ½ cup barbecue sauce and hot pepper sauce; mix well. Serve in rolls.

TAVERN BURGER

• makes 8 servings •

- 2 pounds ground beef
- ½ cup ketchup
- ¼ cup packed brown sugar
- ¼ cup yellow mustard
- Hamburger buns

1 Brown beef in medium skillet over medium-high heat 6 to 8 minutes, stirring to break up meat. Drain fat. Transfer beef to slow cooker.

2 Add ketchup, brown sugar and mustard to slow cooker; mix well. Cover and cook on LOW 4 to 6 hours. Serve on buns.

CHUNKY RANCH POTATOES

• makes 8 servings •

- 3 pounds unpeeled red potatoes, quartered
- 1 cup water
- ½ teaspoon salt
- ½ cup ranch dressing
- ½ cup grated Parmesan or Cheddar cheese
- ¼ cup minced fresh chives

1 Place potatoes, water and salt in slow cooker. Cover and cook on LOW 7 to 9 hours or on HIGH 4 to 6 hours or until potatoes are tender.

2 Stir in ranch dressing, cheese and chives. Break up potatoes into chunks.

CHANNA CHAT (INDIAN-SPICED SNACK MIX)

• makes 6 to 8 servings •

2 teaspoons canola oil
1 medium onion, finely chopped, divided
2 cloves garlic, minced
2 cans (about 15 ounces each) chickpeas, rinsed and drained
¼ cup vegetable broth or water
2 teaspoons tomato paste
¼ teaspoon ground cinnamon
¼ teaspoon ground cumin
¼ teaspoon black pepper
1 bay leaf
½ cup balsamic vinegar
1 tablespoon brown sugar
1 plum tomato, chopped
½ jalapeño pepper, minced *or* ¼ teaspoon ground red pepper (optional)
½ cup crisp rice cereal
3 tablespoons chopped fresh cilantro (optional)

1 Heat oil in small skillet over medium heat. Add half of onion and garlic; cook and stir 2 minutes or until softened. Transfer to slow cooker. Stir chickpeas, broth, tomato paste, cinnamon, cumin, black pepper and bay leaf into slow cooker.

2 Cover and cook on LOW 6 hours or on HIGH 3 hours. Remove and discard bay leaf.

3 Transfer chickpeas to large bowl with slotted spoon; let cool 15 minutes. Meanwhile, combine balsamic vinegar and brown sugar in small saucepan. Cook over medium-low heat until mixture becomes syrupy.

4 Stir tomato, remaining onion and jalapeño, if desired, into chickpeas. Fold in rice cereal and drizzle with balsamic syrup. Garnish with cilantro.

CHICKEN AND ASIAGO STUFFED MUSHROOMS

• makes 4 to 5 servings •

- 20 large white mushrooms, stems removed and reserved
- 3 tablespoons olive oil, divided
- ¼ cup finely chopped onion
- 2 cloves garlic, minced
- ¼ cup Madeira wine
- ½ pound chicken sausage, casings removed, or ground chicken
- 1 cup grated Asiago cheese
- ¼ cup seasoned Italian bread crumbs
- 3 tablespoons finely chopped fresh parsley
- ½ teaspoon salt
- ¼ teaspoon black pepper

1. Remove stems from mushrooms; finely chop. Lightly brush mushroom caps with 1 tablespoon oil.
2. Heat remaining 2 tablespoons oil in large nonstick skillet over medium-high heat. Add onion; cook and stir 1 minute. Add mushroom stems; cook and stir 5 to 6 minutes or until beginning to brown. Stir in garlic; cook 1 minute. Add wine; cook 1 minute or until evaporated.
3. Add sausage; cook 3 to 4 minutes until no longer pink, stirring to break up meat. Remove from heat; cool 5 minutes. Stir in cheese, bread crumbs, parsley, salt and pepper. Divide sausage mixture among mushroom caps, pressing slightly to compress. Place mushrooms in single layer in slow cooker.
4. Cover and cook on LOW 4 hours or on HIGH 2 hours or until mushrooms are tender and filling is cooked through.

STUFFED BABY BELL PEPPERS

• makes 16 to 18 servings •

- 1 tablespoon olive oil
- ½ medium onion, chopped
- ½ pound ground beef, chicken or turkey
- ½ cup cooked rice
- 3 tablespoons finely chopped fresh parsley
- 2 tablespoons lemon juice
- 1 tablespoon dried dill weed
- 1 tablespoon tomato paste, divided
- ½ teaspoon salt
- ⅛ teaspoon black pepper
- 1 package mini sweet peppers (about 24 peppers)
- ¼ cup vegetable, chicken or beef broth

1 Heat oil in medium skillet over medium heat. Add onion; cook and stir 5 minutes or until translucent.

2 Add beef; cook 6 to 8 minutes or until browned, stirring to break up meat. Drain fat. Transfer to large bowl. Add rice, parsley, lemon juice, dill weed, 1½ teaspoons tomato paste, salt and black pepper; mix well.

3 Cut small slit in side of each pepper; run under cold water to wash out seeds. Fill each pepper with 2 to 3 teaspoons beef mixture. Place peppers in slow cooker, slit side up. Whisk broth and remaining 1½ teaspoons tomato paste in small bowl until well blended. Add to slow cooker. Cover and cook on LOW 5 hours or on HIGH 2½ hours.

THAI COCONUT CHICKEN MEATBALLS

• makes 4 to 5 servings •

1 pound ground chicken
2 green onions, chopped
1 clove garlic, minced
2 teaspoons toasted sesame oil
2 teaspoons mirin
1 teaspoon fish sauce
1 tablespoon vegetable oil

½ cup unsweetened canned coconut milk
¼ cup chicken broth
2 teaspoons packed brown sugar
1 teaspoon Thai red curry paste
2 teaspoons lime juice
2 tablespoons water
1 tablespoon cornstarch

1 Combine chicken, green onions, garlic, sesame oil, mirin and fish sauce in large bowl. Shape into 1½-inch meatballs.

2 Heat vegetable oil in large skillet over medium-high heat. Working in batches, brown meatballs on all sides. Transfer to slow cooker. Add coconut milk, broth, brown sugar and curry paste. Cover and cook on HIGH 3½ to 4 hours. Stir in lime juice.

3 Stir water into cornstarch in small bowl until smooth; stir into slow cooker. Cook, uncovered, on HIGH 10 to 15 minutes or until sauce is slightly thickened.

LEMON CAULIFLOWER

• makes 6 servings •

1 tablespoon butter

3 cloves garlic, minced

½ cup water

2 tablespoons lemon juice

4 tablespoons chopped fresh Italian parsley, divided

1 teaspoon salt

½ teaspoon grated lemon peel

6 cups (about 1½ pounds) cauliflower florets

¼ cup grated Parmesan cheese

Lemon wedges (optional)

1 Melt butter in small saucepan over medium heat. Add garlic; cook and stir 2 to 3 minutes or until soft. Stir in water, lemon juice, 1 tablespoon parsley, salt and lemon peel. Pour into slow cooker.

2 Add cauliflower; stir to blend. Cover and cook on LOW 4 hours.

3 Sprinkle with remaining 3 tablespoons parsley and cheese before serving. Garnish with lemon wedges.

GREEK-STYLE CHICKEN WINGS WITH TZATZIKI SAUCE

• makes 8 servings •

Chicken Wings

- 2 tablespoons olive oil, divided
- 5 pounds chicken wings, tips removed and split at joints
- 2 teaspoons dried oregano
- ½ teaspoon salt
- ¼ teaspoon black pepper
- 2 tablespoons lemon juice

Tzatziki Sauce

- 1 seedless cucumber
- 2 cups plain Greek yogurt
- 2 tablespoons lemon juice
- 2 tablespoons olive oil
- 1 clove garlic, minced
- ½ teaspoon salt

1 Heat 1 tablespoon oil in large nonstick skillet over medium-high heat. Working in batches, cook chicken about 6 minutes or until browned on both sides. Place in slow cooker.

2 Sprinkle oregano over chicken. Drizzle with 1 tablespoon olive oil and toss gently to coat. Cover and cook on HIGH 3 to 3½ hours or until tender. Sprinkle with ½ teaspoon salt and pepper and drizzle with 2 tablespoons lemon juice. Toss gently to coat.

3 Meanwhile for tzatziki sauce, peel cucumber and grate on large holes of box grater into large bowl. Stir in yogurt, 2 tablespoons lemon juice, 2 tablespoons olive oil, garlic and ½ teaspoon salt. Cover and refrigerate until ready to use. Serve with chicken wings.

GARDEN POTATO CASSEROLE

• makes 4 to 6 servings •

- 1¼ pounds unpeeled baking potatoes, thinly sliced
- 1 green or red bell pepper, thinly sliced
- ¼ cup finely chopped yellow onion
- 2 tablespoons butter, cut into small pieces, divided
- ½ teaspoon dried thyme
- Salt and black pepper
- 1 small yellow squash, thinly sliced
- 1 cup (4 ounces) shredded sharp Cheddar cheese

1. Place potatoes, bell pepper, onion, 1 tablespoon butter and thyme in slow cooker. Season with salt and black pepper; mix well. Layer squash over top; dot with remaining 1 tablespoon butter.
2. Cover and cook on LOW 7 hours or on HIGH 4 hours.
3. Transfer vegetables to serving bowl. Sprinkle with cheese; let stand 2 to 3 minutes or until cheese is melted.

BACON-MOLASSES BAKED BEANS

• makes 12 servings •

1 pound dried small white beans (such as Great Northern or navy beans)
1 onion, finely chopped
8 ounces bacon, finely chopped
⅓ cup molasses
¼ cup packed dark brown sugar
2 teaspoons ground mustard
¼ teaspoon black pepper
1½ teaspoons salt

1. Rinse beans in colander under cold water; discard any stones and shriveled beans. Transfer to large bowl; add enough water to cover beans by 2 inches. Cover and let soak overnight. Drain and rinse.
2. Stir beans, onion, bacon, molasses, brown sugar, ground mustard and pepper in slow cooker. Add enough water to cover with 1 inch of water.
3. Cover and cook on LOW 8 hours or until beans are tender and sauce is thickened. Stir in salt.

CAPONATA

• makes about 5¼ cups •

- 1 medium eggplant (about 1 pound), peeled and cut into ½-inch pieces
- 1 can (about 14 ounces) diced Italian plum tomatoes
- 1 onion, chopped
- 1 red bell pepper, cut into ½-inch pieces
- ½ cup salsa
- ¼ cup olive oil
- 2 tablespoons capers, drained
- 2 tablespoons balsamic vinegar
- 3 cloves garlic, minced
- 1 teaspoon dried oregano
- ¼ teaspoon salt
- ⅓ cup packed fresh basil, cut into thin strips
- Toasted Italian or French bread slices

1 Combine eggplant, tomatoes, onion, bell pepper, salsa, oil, capers, vinegar, garlic, oregano and salt in slow cooker. Cover and cook on LOW 7 to 8 hours.

2 Stir in basil. Serve on bread.

LENTILS WITH WALNUTS

• makes 4 to 6 servings •

1 cup brown lentils, rinsed and drained
1 small onion or large shallot, chopped
1 stalk celery, chopped
1 large carrot, chopped
¼ teaspoon dried thyme
3 cups vegetable broth
Salt and black pepper
¼ cup chopped walnuts

1 Combine lentils, onion, celery, carrot and thyme in slow cooker. Pour in broth. Cover and cook on HIGH 3 hours. Do not overcook. (Lentils should absorb most or all of broth. Slightly tilt slow cooker to check.)

2 Season to taste with salt and pepper. Spoon lentils into serving bowl; sprinkle with walnuts.

POLENTA-STYLE CORN CASSEROLE

• makes 6 servings •

- 1 can (about 14 ounces) vegetable broth
- ½ cup cornmeal
- 1 can (7 ounces) corn, drained
- 1 can (4 ounces) diced green chiles, drained
- ¼ cup diced red bell pepper
- ½ teaspoon salt
- ¼ teaspoon black pepper
- 1 cup (4 ounces) shredded Cheddar cheese

1 Pour broth into slow cooker; whisk in cornmeal. Stir in corn, chiles, bell pepper, salt and black pepper. Cover and cook on LOW 4 to 5 hours or on HIGH 2 to 3 hours.

2 Stir in cheese; let stand until melted.

BACON-WRAPPED FINGERLING POTATOES

• makes 4 to 6 servings •

1 pound fingerling potatoes

2 tablespoons olive oil

1 tablespoon minced fresh thyme, plus additional for garnish

½ teaspoon black pepper

¼ teaspoon paprika

8 ounces bacon

¼ cup chicken broth

1 Toss potatoes with oil, 1 tablespoon thyme, pepper and paprika in large bowl.

2 Cut each bacon slice in half lengthwise; wrap half slice of bacon tightly around each potato.

3 Heat large skillet over medium heat; add potatoes. Reduce heat to medium-low; cook until lightly browned and bacon has tightened around potatoes.

4 Place potatoes in slow cooker. Add broth. Cover and cook on HIGH 3 hours or until potatoes are tender. Garnish with additional thyme.

CHORIZO AND CORN DRESSING

• makes 4 to 6 servings •

- 8 ounces chorizo sausage, casings removed
- 1 can (about 14 ounces) chicken broth
- 1 can (10½ ounces) cream of chicken soup
- 1 package (6 ounces) corn bread stuffing mix
- 1 cup chopped onion
- 1 cup diced red bell pepper
- 1 cup chopped celery
- 1 cup frozen corn
- 3 eggs, lightly beaten

1 Spray inside of slow cooker with nonstick cooking spray.

2 Cook chorizo in large skillet over medium-high heat until browned, stirring to break up meat. Transfer to slow cooker.

3 Whisk broth and soup into drippings in skillet. Add stuffing mix, onion, bell pepper, celery, corn and eggs; stir until well blended. Stir into slow cooker. Cover and cook on LOW 7 hours or on HIGH 3½ hours.

SWEET AND SPICY SAUSAGE ROUNDS

• makes about 16 servings •

- 1 pound kielbasa sausage, cut into ¼-inch-thick rounds
- ⅔ cup blackberry jam
- ⅓ cup steak sauce
- 1 tablespoon yellow mustard
- ½ teaspoon ground allspice

Place all ingredients in slow cooker; toss to coat. Cover and cook on HIGH 3 hours or until richly glazed.

RUSTIC CHEDDAR MASHED POTATOES

• makes 8 servings •

- 2 pounds russet potatoes, peeled and diced
- 1 cup water
- ⅓ cup butter, cut into pieces
- ½ to ¾ cup milk
- 1¼ teaspoons salt
- ½ teaspoon black pepper
- ¾ cup (3 ounces) shredded Cheddar cheese
- ½ cup finely chopped green onions

1 Combine potatoes and water in slow cooker; dot with butter. Cover and cook on LOW 6 hours or on HIGH 3 hours or until potatoes are tender. Remove potatoes to large mixing bowl.

2 Beat potatoes with electric mixer at medium speed until fluffy. Add milk, salt and pepper; beat until smooth.

3 Stir in cheese and green onions. Cover and let stand 15 minutes to allow flavors to blend and cheese to melt.

CHEESY CORN AND PEPPERS

• makes 8 servings •

- 2 pounds frozen corn
- 2 poblano peppers, chopped *or* 1 green bell pepper and 1 jalapeño pepper, seeded and finely chopped
- 2 tablespoons butter, cut into small pieces
- 1 teaspoon salt
- ½ teaspoon ground cumin
- ¼ teaspoon black pepper
- 1 cup (4 ounces) shredded sharp Cheddar cheese
- 3 ounces cream cheese, cubed

1 Spray inside of slow cooker with nonstick cooking spray. Add corn, poblanos, butter, salt, cumin and black pepper. Cover and cook on HIGH 2 hours.

2 Add Cheddar cheese and cream cheese; stir to blend. Cover and cook 15 minutes or until cheeses are melted.

SPICED SWEET POTATOES

• makes 4 servings •

- 2 pounds sweet potatoes, peeled and cut into ½-inch pieces
- ¼ cup packed dark brown sugar
- 1 teaspoon ground cinnamon
- ½ teaspoon ground nutmeg
- ¼ teaspoon salt
- 2 tablespoons butter, cut into small pieces
- 1 teaspoon vanilla

1 Combine potatoes, brown sugar, cinnamon, nutmeg and salt in slow cooker; mix well. Cover and cook on LOW 7 hours or on HIGH 4 hours.

2 Add butter and vanilla; gently stir to blend.

Sweet Treats

MIXED BERRY COBBLER

• makes 8 servings •

- 1 package (16 ounces) frozen mixed berries
- ¾ cup granulated sugar
- 2 tablespoons quick-cooking tapioca
- 2 teaspoons grated lemon peel
- 1½ cups all-purpose flour
- ½ cup packed brown sugar
- 2¼ teaspoons baking powder
- ¼ teaspoon salt
- ¼ teaspoon ground nutmeg
- ¾ cup milk
- ⅓ cup butter, melted
- Vanilla ice cream (optional)

1. Combine berries, granulated sugar, tapioca and lemon peel in slow cooker; toss to coat.
2. Combine flour, brown sugar, baking powder, salt and nutmeg in medium bowl. Add milk and butter; stir just until blended. Drop dough by spoonfuls onto berry mixture.
3. Cover and cook on LOW 4 hours. Uncover; let stand 30 minutes. Serve with ice cream, if desired.

APPLE CRUMBLE POT

• makes 6 to 8 servings •

- 1 cup plus 2 tablespoons biscuit baking mix, divided
- 1 cup packed dark brown sugar, divided
- 1½ teaspoons ground cinnamon
- ¼ teaspoon ground allspice
- 4 Granny Smith apples (about 2 pounds), cored and cut into 8 wedges each
- ½ cup dried cranberries
- 5 tablespoons cold butter, cut into small pieces, divided
- 1 teaspoon vanilla
- ½ cup old-fashioned oats
- ½ cup chopped pecans
- Whipped cream (optional)

1 Spray inside of slow cooker with nonstick cooking spray. Combine 2 tablespoons baking mix, ⅔ cup brown sugar, cinnamon and allspice in large bowl; mix well. Add apples, cranberries, 2 tablespoons butter and vanilla; toss gently to coat. Spoon into slow cooker.

2 Combine remaining 1 cup baking mix, ⅓ cup brown sugar and oats in large bowl; mix well. Cut in remaining 3 tablespoons butter with pastry blender or fingertips until mixture resembles coarse crumbs. Sprinkle evenly over fruit mixture in slow cooker. Top with pecans.

3 Cover and cook on HIGH 2 hours or until apples are tender. Turn off heat. Let stand, uncovered, 15 to 30 minutes before serving. Top with whipped cream, if desired.

CHOCOLATE-STUFFED SLOW COOKER FRENCH TOAST

• makes 6 servings •

6 slices (¾-inch-thick) day-old challah or brioche
½ cup semisweet chocolate chips
6 eggs
3 cups half-and-half
⅔ cup granulated sugar
1 teaspoon vanilla
¼ teaspoon salt
Powdered sugar or warm maple syrup
Fresh fruit (optional)

1 Generously butter 2½-quart baking dish that fits inside 6-quart slow cooker. Arrange two bread slices in bottom of dish. Sprinkle with ¼ cup chocolate chips. Add two more bread slices. Sprinkle with remaining ¼ cup chocolate chips. Top with remaining two bread slices.

2 Beat eggs in large bowl. Stir in half-and-half, granulated sugar, vanilla and salt; pour over bread layers. Press bread into liquid. Set aside 10 minutes or until bread has absorbed liquid. Cover dish with buttered foil, butter-side down.

3 Pour 1 inch of hot water into slow cooker. Add baking dish. Cover and cook on HIGH 3 hours or until toothpick inserted into center comes out clean. Remove dish from slow cooker; let stand 10 minutes. Sprinkle with powdered sugar and garnish with fresh fruit.

OATMEAL CRÈME BRÛLÉE

• makes 4 to 6 servings •

4 cups boiling water
3 cups quick oats
½ teaspoon salt
6 egg yolks
½ cup granulated sugar
2 cups whipping cream
1 teaspoon vanilla
¼ cup packed brown sugar

1. Spray inside of slow cooker with nonstick cooking spray. Pour water into slow cooker. Stir in oats and salt; cover.
2. Whisk egg yolks and granulated sugar in medium bowl until well blended. Heat cream and vanilla in medium saucepan over medium heat until small bubbles form around edge of pan. *Do not boil.* Remove from heat. Whisk ½ cup hot cream into egg yolk mixture until blended.* Whisk warmed egg mixture back into cream until blended. Spoon mixture over oatmeal. *Do not stir.*
3. Line lid with two paper towels. Cover and cook on LOW 3 to 3½ hours or until custard is set.
4. Sprinkle brown sugar over surface of custard. Line lid with two dry paper towels. Cover and cook on LOW 10 to 15 minutes or until brown sugar is melted.

**Place bowl on damp towel to prevent slipping.*

APPLE-PECAN BREAD PUDDING

• makes 8 servings •

- 8 cups bread cubes
- 3 cups Granny Smith apples, cubed
- 1 cup chopped pecans
- 8 eggs
- 1 can (12 ounces) evaporated milk
- 1 cup packed brown sugar
- ½ cup apple cider or apple juice
- 2 teaspoons ground cinnamon
- 1 teaspoon ground nutmeg
- 1 teaspoon vanilla
- ½ teaspoon salt
- ½ teaspoon ground allspice
- Vanilla ice cream and caramel topping (optional)

1 Spray inside of slow cooker with nonstick cooking spray. Add bread cubes, apples and pecans.

2 Whisk eggs, evaporated milk, brown sugar, apple cider, cinnamon, nutmeg, vanilla, salt and allspice in large bowl until well blended. Pour over bread mixture in slow cooker.

3 Cover and cook on LOW 3 hours. Serve with ice cream and caramel topping, if desired.

VANILLA SOUR CREAM CHEESECAKE

• makes 6 to 8 servings •

- ¾ cup graham cracker crumbs
- ¼ cup plus 3 tablespoons sugar, divided
- ¼ teaspoon ground nutmeg
- 2 tablespoons butter, melted
- 1 package (8 ounces) cream cheese, softened
- 2 eggs
- ¼ cup sour cream
- 1½ teaspoons vanilla
- 1½ tablespoons all-purpose flour
- Fresh strawberries, sliced (optional)

1 Combine graham cracker crumbs, 1 tablespoon sugar and nutmeg in medium bowl. Stir in butter until well blended. Press mixture onto bottom and 1 inch up side of 7-inch springform pan.

2 Beat cream cheese in large bowl with electric mixer at high speed 3 to 4 minutes or until smooth. Add remaining ¼ cup plus 2 tablespoons sugar; beat 1 to 2 minutes or until fluffy. Beat in eggs, sour cream and vanilla until blended. Stir in flour. Pour batter into crust.

3 Fill 6-quart slow cooker with ½ inch of water and set small wire rack in bottom. Set cheesecake on rack. Line lid with paper towels or clean kitchen towel. Cover and cook on HIGH 2 hours.

4 Turn off heat and let stand 1 hour without opening lid. Remove cheesecake to wire rack; cool completely. Cover with plastic wrap; refrigerate 4 to 5 hours or until cold.

5 To serve, run tip of knife around edge of cheesecake and remove side of pan. Top with strawberries, if desired. Cut into wedges to serve.

PEACH COBBLER

• makes 4 to 6 servings •

- **2 packages (16 ounces each) frozen peaches, thawed and drained**
- **¾ cup plus 1 tablespoon sugar, divided**
- **2 teaspoons ground cinnamon, divided**
- **½ teaspoon ground nutmeg**
- **¾ cup all-purpose flour**
- **6 tablespoons butter, cut into small pieces**
- **Whipped cream (optional)**

1 Combine peaches, ¾ cup sugar, 1½ teaspoons cinnamon and nutmeg in slow cooker.

2 For topping, combine flour, remaining 1 tablespoon sugar and remaining ½ teaspoon cinnamon in small bowl. Cut in butter with pastry blender or fingertips until mixture resembles coarse crumbs. Sprinkle over peach mixture. Cover and cook on HIGH 2 hours. Serve with whipped cream, if desired.

COCONUT RICE PUDDING

• makes 6 servings •

- 2 cups water
- 1 cup uncooked converted long grain rice
- 1 tablespoon butter
- Pinch salt
- 2¼ cups evaporated milk
- 1 can (14 ounces) cream of coconut
- ½ cup golden raisins
- 3 egg yolks, beaten
- Grated peel of 2 limes
- 1 teaspoon vanilla
- Toasted shredded coconut (optional)

1 Bring water, rice, butter and salt to a boil in medium saucepan over high heat, stirring frequently. Reduce heat to low; cover and cook 10 minutes. Remove from heat. Let stand, covered, 5 minutes.

2 Spray inside of slow cooker with nonstick cooking spray. Add evaporated milk, cream of coconut, raisins, egg yolks, lime peel and vanilla; mix well. Add rice; stir until blended.

3 Cover and cook on LOW 4 hours or on HIGH 2 hours, stirring every 30 minutes, if possible. Pudding will thicken as it cools. Garnish with toasted coconut, if desired.

APPLE-DATE CRISP

• makes 6 servings •

6 cups thinly sliced peeled tart apples (about 6 medium)
2 teaspoons lemon juice
⅓ cup chopped dates
1⅓ cups quick oats
½ cup all-purpose flour
½ cup packed brown sugar
½ teaspoon ground cinnamon
¼ teaspoon ground ginger
¼ teaspoon salt
Dash ground nutmeg
Dash ground cloves (optional)
¼ cup (½ stick) cold butter, cut into small pieces

1 Spray inside of slow cooker with nonstick cooking spray. Place apples in slow cooker. Sprinkle with lemon juice; toss to coat. Stir in dates.

2 Combine oats, flour, brown sugar, cinnamon, ginger, salt, nutmeg and cloves, if desired, in medium bowl. Cut in butter with pastry blender or fingertips until mixture resembles coarse crumbs.

3 Sprinkle oat mixture over apples; smooth top. Cover and cook on LOW 4 hours or on HIGH 2 hours or until apples are tender.

BANANA-RUM CUSTARD

• makes 4 to 6 servings •

1½ cups milk
3 eggs
½ cup sugar
3 tablespoons dark rum or milk
⅛ teaspoon salt
1 medium banana, sliced ¼ inch thick
15 to 18 vanilla wafers

1 Whisk milk, eggs, sugar, rum and salt in medium bowl. Pour into 1-quart baking dish that fits inside slow cooker. Do not cover.

2 Place rack in slow cooker and pour in 1 cup water. Place baking dish on rack. Cover and cook on LOW 3½ to 4 hours.

3 Remove baking dish from slow cooker. Spoon custard into dessert dishes. Arrange banana slices and wafers over custard.

DECADENT CHOCOLATE DELIGHT

• makes 12 servings •

1 package (about 15 ounces) chocolate cake mix

1 cup (8 ounces) sour cream

1 cup semisweet chocolate chips

1 cup water

4 eggs

¾ cup vegetable oil

1 package (4-serving size) chocolate instant pudding and pie filling mix

Vanilla ice cream

1 Spray inside of slow cooker with nonstick cooking spray.

2 Combine cake mix, sour cream, chocolate chips, water, eggs, oil and pudding mix in large bowl; mix well. Transfer to slow cooker.

3 Cover and cook on LOW 3 to 4 hours or on HIGH 1½ to 1¾ hours. Serve warm with ice cream.

Index

Index

Index

Index

METRIC CONVERSION CHART

VOLUME MEASUREMENTS (dry)

1/8 teaspoon = 0.5 mL
1/4 teaspoon = 1 mL
1/2 teaspoon = 2 mL
3/4 teaspoon = 4 mL
1 teaspoon = 5 mL
1 tablespoon = 15 mL
2 tablespoons = 30 mL
1/4 cup = 60 mL
1/3 cup = 75 mL
1/2 cup = 125 mL
2/3 cup = 150 mL
3/4 cup = 175 mL
1 cup = 250 mL
2 cups = 1 pint = 500 mL
3 cups = 750 mL
4 cups = 1 quart = 1 L

VOLUME MEASUREMENTS (fluid)

1 fluid ounce (2 tablespoons) = 30 mL
4 fluid ounces (1/2 cup) = 125 mL
8 fluid ounces (1 cup) = 250 mL
12 fluid ounces (1 1/2 cups) = 375 mL
16 fluid ounces (2 cups) = 500 mL

WEIGHTS (mass)

1/2 ounce = 15 g
1 ounce = 30 g
3 ounces = 90 g
4 ounces = 120 g
8 ounces = 225 g
10 ounces = 285 g
12 ounces = 360 g
16 ounces = 1 pound = 450 g

DIMENSIONS

1/16 inch = 2 mm
1/8 inch = 3 mm
1/4 inch = 6 mm
1/2 inch = 1.5 cm
3/4 inch = 2 cm
1 inch = 2.5 cm

OVEN TEMPERATURES

250°F = 120°C
275°F = 140°C
300°F = 150°C
325°F = 160°C
350°F = 180°C
375°F = 190°C
400°F = 200°C
425°F = 220°C
450°F = 230°C

BAKING PAN SIZES

Utensil	Size in Inches/Quarts	Metric Volume	Size in Centimeters
Baking or Cake Pan (square or rectangular)	8×8×2	2 L	20×20×5
	9×9×2	2.5 L	23×23×5
	12×8×2	3 L	30×20×5
	13×9×2	3.5 L	33×23×5
Loaf Pan	8×4×3	1.5 L	20×10×7
	9×5×3	2 L	23×13×7
Round Layer Cake Pan	8×1½	1.2 L	20×4
	9×1½	1.5 L	23×4
Pie Plate	8×1¼	750 mL	20×3
	9×1¼	1 L	23×3
Baking Dish or Casserole	1 quart	1 L	—
	1½ quart	1.5 L	—
	2 quart	2 L	—